Flesh Phoenix

MITCH GREEN

Re issue

Copyright © Rad Press Publishing/ Second Edition
Mitch Green

Flesh Phoenix

All rights reserved. No part of this publication may be reproduced, distributed or conveyed without the permission of the author or publisher.

Cover design/Interior design by Mitch Green

She's a flesh phoenix. A stratospheric bombshell.

I

Venus

The muse
mileage.

*Venus is
hemorrhaging*

The skewering
stain of
dichotomy.

*Venus is
hemorrhaging*

A peripheral
parabola of
missionary.

*Venus is
hemorrhaging*

The razor wrists
cuffed behind
the back of
Mother Nature.

*Venus is
hemorrhaging.*

The ventricle
idle idols in
wax and spears.

*Venus is
hemorrhaging*

Centipede
therapy; entity
purity.

*Venus is
hemorrhaging*

Plant Our Bones

This is sacrilegiously staged.
Slathered and slandered in segments –
inverted, extorted discretely,
secreting symptomizing points of
interest. We are retorting
resplendence as if it
came upon us to repent
our self-made sins.

Picturing places we've been –
gone or going, in this
intersecting detail of
debauched deliverance.
We wait for our weight to
make the first move. The
interlude, the opening act.
The prologue where decaying
dispositions position the
lucky ones the privilege
to scarf in tranquility.

Take a breath.
Shuttle the shy.
Harvest the sky, for
we coincide collectively
off of partnering highs.
Mindless. Mildewed.
We've been here hope
building and faith
funding, while the
while and everlasting
skips town to profit off
of other planets –
near and a lot less
mild, than this wild
wide world we plant
our bones in.

Floating Facedown

I'm a floatation in a
fluid sky, spreading
my muscled halo
around the rim of
the universe, upon,
as beauty beats on,
I will capture prisms
behind these eyes to
stream projections of
spectral explosions
splashing shades
to color the faithless
atmosphere.

Wet Salt

Your cold, wet warmth,
sliding down the arch
of my hips. A rolling
intolerable sensation
shaking to bend a
quivering satisfaction
to dampen the spoils of my
inner thighs. There's
nothing quite like the
way you move your lips
to tongue a feeling into
my bones.

Cautiously around
you work your body,
an engine of arousal
to stem and stir the
throes of your demands.
Like wet dogs, we shake
the salt from skin, and
connect our weight,
interrogating the
intimacy with a
submissive coil.
Recoiling conscious
foreplay to evolve into
a curling of toes and
knuckles. White knuckled,
knees buckling. Clutch
wars. In between the
divide of your faith,
I find a salvation.

There Are Monsters In Heaven

We ran out, away from
all the things that would
cause us harm. We left
the lights in our old homes
on, but filched the décor.
Countless, we counted the
streets, and all the bed
sheets we burned. Our lives,
they are changing, and
we're leaving, behind the low
times, for a wild fire.
In a wild life, my darling,
tonight, let's burn.

Angelic Alienation

We flicker in on an upside-
down spell spaced room.
Decorations enveloping –
revolving normality.
Neatly noxious, teasingly
tasteless – facing from
ceiling to an unmade mattress,
exists also an unlaced,
leisurely lying lady. Sultry wear.
Bastardizing beauty in
diluted dictation of some
racy simulation of cute
and damaged. Battle black
bruises, swollen skeletal
contusions – perforations,
aftermath of a bomb
blasted illusion. Made of
realism for play.

Praising her buoyancy;
made to sway upward into
our cosmic correlation.
She spaces her fingers in
fabrications, signaling
the enraged and estranged
prodigies from the strange
faith of falling face down.
Rising. Climaxing.
Counting in reverse.
Possessed princess in
nothing but her waxen world.
Closer to our lips. To our
reality. To our mental. To
the severity of our
principle. Possible to taste,
to touch, to fuck – she

orbits our abortion
of existential innocence.
Invasive, intrusive,
elusive interference of
vanity in physical sobriety.
She unwinds her tongue to
charm, to harm, to alarm,
to invigorate us. Her
sexuality shadows our
partnership. We are the
procreative prequel
for preview.
She's the perversion
of perfection,
but perfectly
persuading
perversion.

Savior

Remember that night? When In the heights
of midnight - out of touch with ourselves,
we touched each other. We are the audience,
the distinctive identity of various and
vast voices whistling through the
cracked windows. We know nothing
but on how to make waves in this
mechanical jungle. Seats become
handbrakes. Head space stolen off
of infusion. Torn muscles,
bloodshot eyes, descending teeth,
hands like silver razors reacting
out of impulse. The sounds are ungodly,
like some grating war between chalk
and glass. Our backseat windshield
reflects gravitating sweat.
Shuffling. Rolling. Rambling.
Bending. Breaking.
Twisting. Spinning.
Exchanging.
Romanticizing the
idea of how we are all
simply spiritual.
Nothing normal ever
comes out this far -
this deep away from
a world where belonging
is seen as something you
can call your own.
We are all alone.
Living, loving,
fighting, and
feeling in ways
that explore
the behavior of
our self-serving savior.

Dance Devil, Dance

Flicker in on the face of a car hood.
Fierce fog lights spitting smoke to
swivel and scale the spine of a
feminine fragility. Fractured
at each jointed connection.
Dancing diva, demonstrative doer of
dares. She's the kind of apparition
who causes cars to crash.
Palms against wiper-bladed glass.
Knees knocking notches into our hood.
Heavy hitter of front seat spectators,
we, the wheelmen of retrospective,
spare attention to this wiry, spirited
spectacle. Four legged seater,
sweet scented cheater.
She shares with us her burning burdens.
Her various personal virginities.
Her stage act.
Her culture.
Her primitive provisions.
Cash crimped to sizzle deep
beneath teeth that grip.
Wet woman of transgressional aggression.
Lock the doors from the outside, she says.
Lock us up tight in our suits and
tied wrists. Buckled to the leather.
We're going nowhere. Fiendish fetish.
Soon we'll be one of the same.
There's a blackout in her grimace.
A smile so vile it could filch the
enamel to escape our gums.
We were warned. We were given a shot.

Two mixed
drinks down.
Devil hot.
Hell handed us a savior,
and we forgot how she was
forged of fevers. Sweating,
we couldn't cool. Contemporarily
contrite, oxygen divorced us.
Inhalation of red gloss fumes
concocted in perfume.
So strong, even throughout
the emblazoned gasoline
waves; our senses caved.

Oceanic Highways

I could tell you
just exactly how
far I would go to
meet you.

At odd hours,
in odd places.

Where purple
eyes bleed.

I could show you
the invisible silk
stretched atop
vanilla textures
told to unfurl, as
does arms on
oceanic highways.

Inertia

The night grew deeper
as around me she moved,
smoking grey, warped
in absolution, hinged
over and glued together
in motion. She's open,
but a burning ocean,
and I'm swimming in
circles, learning what
kind of a god could
invent such inertia.

Limber Listener

Levitating on a dome,
a scalped circle of parted hair
presents itself at our waist.
Our perception is
perpendicular to how
this figure is merged
comfortably. Naturally
nipped and cropped to fit
the mix of our mass.
Knuckled imposters invade,
score the white flesh of her
microwaveable cranium.
She is the damsel of delicacy.
Articulation of abnormality.
Different, but differently
delicate. She's wispy. A fiber.
Limber limbed listener,
with an ear soaking up
the secreting secrets
of what makes us whole.
She's melting liquid.
A vapor in a whiteout.
A pale perversion of
what makes perfect,
perfect.

Glass Gods

We've seen the day sink
to night. Leaves shift
shades of autumn burn.
Swell and deflate to fall.
A cosmic saloon of furnace
springs melting into a
miasma. Fading in. The trees.
The gardens sprite in decay.
Glass Gods gleaming through
gloss windows.
We are not of this place.
Perceptions of presences
only to furnish;
fornicate the formulations
of a sealed spherical stage.
Human homes owning
invertebrate invaders.
Last on earth.
In a cubic contortion
of contouring
calibrations.
Like a luminous
lustrous leviathan
leering through
plaster pixilation,
we were born this way.

Lost and strange.

Bite Open The Scar

Discovered out of bounds,
and blending slightly
shattered, you were caught
touching the sides of us
that were lethally loud.
Surface surfer, cautiously
closed off to others like
me, but I suppose you
swore on it all that it was
always meant to be this
intricate. This wild. This
free. This overwhelming.
This long living. This tamed.
This damaged. This pristine.
Caught in a solar ecliptic
crisis, spaced from scalp
to sole, separated cycle of
seen scenes. Your layers led
me deeper, on depth
depletion, and
darker days.
Bite open the scar,
strike the flare,
emboss the calm,
and quench the storm.

Fire. Fire.
Fire away.

At least in flames,
we'll remain warm.

I've never been jealous of lines, shapes and the hue
of the untouchable, until the night she came across
in nothing but the shadows she wore out of habit.

Imprint

We're drifting sideways
through an open space.
Serenely spiraling,
spinning, spooling – mind
swimming in a solution.
Our whereabouts aren't on
location.

Simplistically enough,
we're the solidity of
an ether enamored to invert.
We're collapsing, closing the shade.
Meddling to mingle a mold.
Washed over in a toxic cold,
flooding flush our figure.
Dance we do in the dark,
blindfolded buffoons beveled
black by fragments. Abstractions
of artificial affliction.
We take note. We modify to
bone. We are reborn.
We are no longer the placenta
of rejection. We are the
physical parabola of width
and height. Godlike muses
thawed and bent out of
proportion to placidity.

All made to be made –
swishing sounds splashing,
and we emerge. Our facial
imprint sponges back at us
through the mirror of heat.
After all, we are all atrocious
embodiments masked behind meat.

Lover

Swear to tell me you
believed we'd come
this far away from
nothing and everything,
only to end up in a place
where it is safe to slip
out of our skeletons.

And I will swear on
our skin that this here,
is where we will stay.

Nuclear Nudity

A breath away from hearing a heartbeat over a sleeping shape - we are invasively close. It hums, mumbles, and snores as it sleeps. We see it all. Hear it all. No filter, and no shame. This is art. This is the world in skin. This is life. What are we doing? What are our intentions? How come the window to our left is open? Invasion of entry. Lost morale to obsessional property. These walls do not own our home. These walls are delicate. Fragile. Fixed from the bedroom door to the bedframe. Fiction hasn't the gumption to be this bold. This audacious. This over the top. "Do it now" hammers the set of lips behind my ears. Inside my head, where the customary mind neglects sleep.
The shape settles.
Turns from side to spine.
Move close.
The shape shakes.
It has a sex.
Nudity.
Soft shaven and simple, yet complex.
She is nuclear.
She is alive.
She is the scar left after a burn.
She is dreaming of all the love she lives.
She is dangerously human. She is,
and I am not.

A Kiss From Bedlam

Patiently, playfully,
stationary, and carefully
we collapsed in a moment
of colossal mishaps,
misshapes, and misplacements.
Wrinkling, slinking into
thwarts of prose, poetics
and unconscious love making.

Swim

She was the kind
you could swim in
if only you knew
how to hold your
breath just right.
But I was more a
lover than a swimmer,
therefore I decided
to stay forever.

Soft to Hard

Come crawl me out of
this bed, investigate
the soft to hard bits
that flare a romantic
conflagration. Instantly
combust and let flow
the elements of
your design.
A delicate, demanding
disposition shuddering
my entire physical.
Cut my core gently
in crosses to brand
me yours.

Snubbed

The intuitive, injected illusion insisted on firing away. Out about three miles deep, wide, a wondering wilderness recites how to inhabit a kingdom of interstellar phenomenal proportions.

Perspiring platitudes picking poisonous prey for procreation. A streaming starlit lagoon, leeching loud lovers who go on about eating one another, just until the dawn dances on diamond dirt, and ditches serendipity for sadism.

Cold play culprit, kingpin of collapse. Sheltered dominance, violent venders defending the disturbed. Creepy crawling killers, shooed away in mass. Shoveled beneath a bulking billow of dead willows rolled in roots and grass, so that one and not two could rest lazily in long lapses, without the need for anything unearthly to surface.

Dead in deathly routines, we're walking isles of the obscene. Clinging casually to warm beds in hopes to extract the imperceptible filth we had aborted, go on, away, where the soil stings the cuts we made.

Epitaph

You are the irrevocable
gem of ongoing security.
Every motion that is
mutual to beauty.
I see a world in you.
I see stars, celestial simulations
diverged amongst eons on fire.
Skies sloping to skid epitaphs
worth of iridescent stratospheres,
scattered chaotically in every
hallucinogenic hue.
Valuing your disbanded
illustrative, I had to
take a step back to absorb
in the breathing ritual of
ratification. Because in
all this time, I hadn't
known that oxygen
had a kill switch until I
became coalesced with you.

Hurry Home, Heart

My vessel of fortitude,
chapel of completion, my
spherical craft of idealistic,
perpetual purification.
An exhale in growth of self,
you, the friction and
static, enflaming tantric
ways to nurture my nature.
You name me in roads, traveler,
traversing over treaded
points of attraction, the
windowed walls of my eyes.
A distorted, directional,
distinction, sighting out
into the glass shaped
shell you hold so
well. Splice us into double
sided reflections to
forever face another,
long ways, allotting out the
finite for the infinite,
by the same manner you flesh

yourself.
Myself.
Ourselves.

Equilibrium

I tangle beneath
myself in the roots of her
equilibrium. Transcendence to passage.
Safely, softly, solemnity.
I think of God when I think of her.
Inward staring out, all those
inexplicable solutions
flushing me away.
All the brand new days,
shores, bedsheets, trees,
stars, suns, moons, magnificent
myths, scars, the intake of O,
the exhale of neurotoxins,
and those sleeves she
rolls her hearts with.

Muse

Filtered figure of fervor,
feverishly fragile, my
darling intensive,
vitally ferocious –
faith skim to hover,
hang above this floor.
Oversee this stasis shell,
shattered, shaking,
we've been sinking,
slathered in comas.
An illusory, self –
evolutionary,
invested invitation.
We let the rope slip,
as did we into suspension.
She's love's lyrical
resurrection.

Ghosting

Lightly living in love,
I discovered a god with the
same eyes and thighs as her's.
And death, in all that
dead darkness, all really
seemed alive at first.
But now I'm ghosting about -
happily ever haunted
by her sound.

Cube Circus

We are witness to the
cubed room loud in volume.
The white noise of existing
nature has now expired,
retired to the audible
entombment of a nexus.
A circus it is in here.
Pronunciations power-rolling
together to create babble.
Shelling off the exterior
level of skin. What lies
underneath is hard to
believe. A scale-less,
in-hideous signification.
To stay fighting together,
keeping the fibers pressed
deep into the mortal leather -
she unfolds out to spare the
boiling gold, thinning
through her casing.
Chords pull through chorus
lines of auditory pitch.
Complacent seductions
beneath every niche.

Utopia

Centuries, divinities, infinites, and
perforated dimensional hypocrisies
fictionalize spiritual effigies to
procreate paradoxical utopias.

Cutie

The haze elevates to stoke the ceiling, dispersing to wane from the whips of a zooming fan. It is in the way you see intercourse. It's messy, undignified, unjustly, unruly – a fierce commencement of inaccuracy between two. Shoving, thrusting, pushing through, in the way animals like us behave.

Thirsty, the male protagonist pins his lady lover down. Lively alive, he, with a sandpaper appendage pickled in buds, swabs her perspiring plush husk. She is invigorated and appalled all the same. According to the visualization mocking up a must see, must feel event of carnality. The act ceases to perform.

The weight of the room shifts from two, to one rolled on her side, drafting a cigarette from beneath her pillow, up to her lips. Lights the head, and inhales deeply, as if this was her last chemical intake. The man is one of few words. It would appear that he suffocates his feelings, his expressional vulnerability snuggled underneath the weight of his tongue.

He just sits, thieving a hit from her oral fixation. Huffs, and finishes off the stick of fire. Up, he lifts from the damp, dented mattress. Littered in chaos. She among the mashup, sits, Indian styled, rolling another smoke. Her shambolic, nakedly nostalgically noxious appearance blends naturally into the scene. Glass walls reflect the hulking profile creeping from view.

Alone she sits, left to spit pieces of tobacco off her tongue. Cutie in cold skin, chillingly calm. Anesthetically attached to nothing than the rolling of her thumbs pinching each end of the bud together. Tears teasingly swell behind the padded lids of her irises.

Nose to top lip popping to intensify the sequence of melancholy. The tonic of her blackened cheeks soak the bedsheets. She sniffles. Restores composure, flips the bud in reverse and brands herself. Pressing it. Digging it. Smudging it in deep against her neck.

Clamped jaws. Fingers become black from the smoke. A whimper and then laughter. Bilingually tasteful in a talent of voicing verbs in words outside of normal mediocrity. Lastly, beneath her pillow, beside the Marlboro box, is the handle of a loaded gun. She mothers it maternally, and strokes it lightly. Cuticles scratch it softly, constricting to wrap the trigger. Barrel to bedside burlesque. She directs the directional exorcism at his spine.

Fires.

The room splashes from orange to pink. Reverberations redecorate the walls in red. Shellshock kindles our ears to scream, as smoke and steam mix to screen the scene.

Fossils

Tenderly torqued to warm as I woke.
I experienced waves of oxygen wading
wide from walls of smoke.
Vaporized to stoke a choke,
we danced, like two exposed,
out of clothed, sensually
eloped lovers, leveled over
to highly hover, until our
fossilized fixations
fizzled under.

She's More Than An Entity

Good mornings at noon artistically invite a silhouette starved skeleton inside my bed.

Living, she lies, drafting hemispheres down under lungs to control volume of how her spontaneous layers enliven me.

How hauntingly possessive all of that flesh to charcoal depiction, complexion to dictation digests from her mouth in parabolic hexagrams.

She's an image imagined with infatuation, a contagion in unison of all I've been made out to be.

Sincerely, I'm obviously intoxicated, invigorated, manipulated on her theoretical, and anatomical majesty.

Darling

You're a ghost though,
and although I've grown
to go out of my way to
become whole, I slip to forget
the steps you made across
my back yard to the
window I left open,

but I'll let you know how
you taste when you haunt
me the way you do.
In all you do.
Oh, and how you wooed
forth the moves out of
my exoskeletal groove.
Through, it shows and
shines straight, I will
hypnotize you, my filtered
darling of placidity.

Because, you're my rouse, my
gist, my powerful, flexible
shelling of what it is that
the universe entitles
to be a gift.

Identity

Fluidity flushed our faces to match
the emblazoned matches ripped to
abandon normality. We sit. We stare
in conflagration, on how we are
but blinking distortions behind
the tongue of delusional defilement.
Vaguely bold in pose, she had crowned
queen her reverie, and I, the fallacy
of ethereal sonnets she slit out through
circumcised identity.

I traversed the travesties of her
buttery flesh, tooth and combed
my way down, resounded and riveted,
torching lightly to do the things
I wished I could do to her fragile
increment of inquired invasion.

Displayable, she's the
playable epiphany.
Creases in phased
chins, she chases chills
to chafe religion.

The City Sleeps In Her Head

I had the windows rolled
opposite of up to allow the
estrogen expression to pardon.
Pleasingly petite, she,
peacefully, very carefully
in casual comfortability
previewed that of a
perfect passenger.

One whom I could take home.
You know, drift gone with.

She's a lover who creases
over every selected segment
of leeching longevity,
and when she breathlessly breathes
out of dimension is when I remember
to watch how the painted world of
metabolic color frays into
shapeshifting surrealism.

Continuum

She ricochets illumination
past the rift of an equinox.
Adopting carnalities, spiritualties,
and a physicality known to cut
out palpable continuum.

Out of who or what we think
we need to be, there are
realities where what we really
are feels more feigned than
all the imaginations we believe.

FLESH PHOENIX REISSUE / MITCH GREEN

Volumes

She stood still in broken fragments
of bleeding glass, washed into palms
of home-grown flesh; psychopathic,
necromantic, romantic – lost in mass.

Meddling meaning, mingles with mad hands;
clapping in rhythmic, rhyming pace.
In dreamscapes you thrive.

Real. Mold – casted to hold.
So close to tongue out the taste,
but what of poison?

Sway softly amid the edge
of pragmatic waste, pouring down.

Where conclusive conscious
strays silent, separated from space.

Vermin

Silent seclusive – reclusive vermin.
Radioactive spiders singing sermons.
Caught in the way your eyes caved –
we saved ourselves. Fought for
replication, duplication of all I
had left. Bended bins – boxing in.
Eating the sulfite solution to
trigger allergic ends. Friends
swallowed whole – shallow pasts
forgotten. Again, we are the ones
writing riots - detain our
self-righteous.

Dig up the ocean
Resuscitate wonder
Justify this fire - it
burns no longer.

Each world we've passed under
Hasn't the charm of the one we
squandered – only invisible ghosts
Boasting of better tomorrows.
Phone the paramedic – too little,
too late. Wait and wake to my call.
Your beauty has always been my
reason, my fall.

Learning to live again
seems easier than it sounds.
There are fears at stake –
faith to be found.

Set persistence
Molotov the crown.

Dogma

Grace found face in volumetric
mandrakes vacating, creating –
making memories. Deep seeded
mistakes serving infinity.

Divinity, hand off the trigger –
self-pity. Entities – domesticated
in fire bed cities.

Privative images – primitive
minds, we're all too involved in
our deadbeat grind. Tries repeated,
defeated by fictitious signs.

Times like these I wish you were
my hindsight – reminiscent cry,
inventing rhymes.

A fire-eater, soul-seek and
destroy dogma. Getting our kicks
on the gum-spit drama.

Hit to bash our inner outcast –
vain karma. Wrong a right, proclaim
and fight the cult coma.

Gone home to mass a cure.
Motif a life worth living for.

Extort – divorce and ban the noir.
Rejoice your voice. It makes for
a better world.

Ships & Harlots

I scream her name in vain of sweet
imperfection, you call it a revelation
I call it Armageddon. We're broken from
breaking, drowning in salt, I gave you
my heart, yet you say it's my fault.
Lost beneath the lies, deception and
hate what does it take to escape this
fate? How long have we been here, how
long have we waited? The lines in my
skin have already faded.

So claim the dead.
Pray for tomorrow.
It's hard to breathe in all of her sorrow.

I hear the voices beneath the water,
screaming out, where did we falter?
Voices beneath the water, thrashing
out, drifting farther.

We are lost!

Of ships and harlots. Her face is a ghost and
I am haunted. Please save me now, I'm scared
and alone, I haven't the strength to sail back
home. Drowning under the weight of her lies,
she hadn't the love to say goodbye. These anchors are
heavy, they're pulling me down, Inside the depths of
sunken crowns. Inhale my cries and harvest the tears.
She is the reason for all my fears.

I hear the voices beneath the
harbor, screaming out, where did
we falter? Voices beneath the harbor,
sinking down, breathing water

Ships and harlots!
She's a ghost.
Ships and harlots.
I am haunted.

Verve

Sinners, saints - bone edged proficient damsels.
Rebirthed reunions relishing fortified
foundations of burial worship. To sink,
we embalm our bones, hope, it's not our home.

Nostalgic principles of dreamscapes and saloons,
dividing oceans. Monsoons, grave lagoons.

Open up - dead man sounds; eating floorboards,
wall space and barking hounds.

Stagnant silhouettes in shallow sand -
convergence, contorted round, into backward
faces - lit in dread.

Steadfast to wake, quaking verses. Viral
fallacies proven to procreate pallid pardons
of the malice in gloss houses, spouses sewn
at the seam of mortal dreams.

Fiends find the promise in fractured,
spatter washed mirrors. Crooked, creepy -
screaming things.

On all fours - flapping tongues, legs
lurching, wild teeth chirping, chatters
swallowing fleshed earth.

All is lost and the growls are faded, the
royals rein over the dead and spaded.

1825

I sold out to fade in on golden,
swollen - swallowed years.
Beginning, I'm feeling as if I
belong here.

Underrated, evaluated as less a man
than before. Wanting more for an
incapacitated mind.

Remembrance of your shine.
Headlights bending your fine
edged creation, Illuminating
the crystal daggers from
livid eyes. Whys and how comes,
shift into deadened.

Again I'm bent. Out of place,
misplaced soul. Holding all I
can to keep from losing control.
Be the reason, the solution -
intervention, animosity.
Another decade in captivity,
teases triumphant ends in me.

Dogwood

The dogwood barked,
The fire-grazers sparked.
All in all we felt our
hearts pound and break,
break and shake.
Fake the sake of
thudding normal.

Killers in painted
sneers, smears
clothing scarecrows.
All resurrected for
trouble.

They wore pig snouts,
all upon six foot tall
beam mounts.
Posts shooting
short of a moon.

Soon it would fall,
just as us all,
beneath a
harvest doom.

Vermillion

Red wolves bleeding white linens.
Coached supermodel Gods' finding religion.
Picturesque idolized vermilion virgins.
Speaking in consonants, bestial urchins.
Ceremonial pigments snorting estrogen tonic.

Laconic linguistic intimacy, wooing hypnotic
heresy. Lascivious claw-cut wool, carving,
starving jealousy. Milk-faded heels, and ankles.

Wrists burned in mud. Spaded spirits of
nefarious nomads - consummation flood.
Freckled topography. Spinal, seductive geography.

Submissive tease, poster posers. Prehistoric
revival soaking up fire on worm-earth knees;
analytical survival. Mother morale jaws down
on yawning with moaning throats. Stoking smoke
to asphyxiate toxins, bare ladies wearing goats.

Ominous aristocrats, masked maidens.
Howling and bleeding white linens.
Red wolves fathering dens. Alpha-relations.

Static Elephant

She was silent at first. All but her lips
mouthing phrases. Engorged eyes, filling up
like blue crystal balloons. An infatuated,
pencil and pen scribbled smile.

Simpleton savior.

In every hour I'm failing. Can one so
many be a part of the ordinary? Shadows
hosting sunspots. Alter-egotistic,
testing the prolific. Sensitive silences
slithering into deafness. Communion of
vapor should stand for something.
Post-pardons of previous lovers'.

Lipstick bled covers. We're all growing
in dying skin. Wishing, hoping and
praying for invincibility to be born.
The mind might find a balance
between miracle and menace.

Digested scorn - upchucking
the deep-seeded. Depleted, repeated,
advancing passes to obsessive genus.
Mainstream manic. Tantric panic.
An organic mental. Montage vicious,
awkward kisses. Intimate criminal.

Chameleon

This isn't the way to live, when will
the prayers give? Survive only to be
left behind. We're finding desire to
be set afire. Inhale, choke – these
are my words smothered in smoke.

Mental insecurity, sense of deaf clarity.
Instant severity. For vanity, we've lost
all passage to our sanity. Only the
aftermath pushing out the grey foam,
I wasn't built to manage alone. Through
thick and thin, under the rich and amid
the weak, This'll be the moment
I welcome frustration.

Liberation of my own foiling thoughts.
Back and forth, I'll Colour my demons.
Deep purples to vibrant blues, Either
way, I'll be reminded of you. You're one
in a sea of a billion, shifting tone like
a fucking chameleon. Feeling faithful
to the chemistry, Yet refusing the
symmetry. The silence, violently heard.

Blister the perseverance of an eventual
finality. Agitating the carnality to bite.
Tooth and nail, I'll keep on swinging.
Dreaming, screaming while these walls break.
Post your good intentions. Submit the courage,
Let's reinvent the prevention.

Cease the hurting. Disowning the
person I once was feels like murder.
Cold hands, wet sand,
evolution of a new man.

Mad Meows

While ingesting confessions on borderline biddings.
To renew lease on captured Cthulhus' We'll squander
the chatter of a dead English master, and snuff volatile
bones blown blue.

Cultivating the clockwork owls haunting hollow
grounds in need for fire roasting undead squires.
Depravity defines the gravity these dead head
fans desire. Morbidity musters melancholic muses
to craft and cut reputable attire.

Dreams of mad, unfathomable fiends find playground
in these skeletal streets. Whilst creep beggars scarf
the barf from hoofed boots, digesting mortality.

It's an ode to passage, unto the deepest, darkest
valleys of horror. Swept crypts of cryptic courtyard
law. For what master craft had saw were illusionary
depictions of vile reflections.

Master of mind-warping visions, all but conflicting
his conditions. A meowing menace to forge these
towers of ancient finish. Historical fictions.

Starfish

We're contemporary - temporarily plain and vain.
Yet, what I see in her could be misinterpreted,
mistaken as interrupted perfection. A complicated
blessing, driven wild with affection.

Part art, part shark. I'm second guessing
the trade mark she left on my heart.

20th

I spent my twentieth
on Twentieth Street.
Beaten between twenty
tepid tiffs, and bent
beneath twenty stories
of tension. No longer
addicted, although
ashamed of commitment.
I paid my spirit with dues
of attention and
loved every minute.

Squares

Reciting foreplay from porno
verses – kicking curbs in bloody
converses. Television boxes
televising 50's medicine.
Old western depression – seducing
sessions for clinical confessions.
Inside from the wolfing cries of
breaking magic. We're all sinners
strung out on bad habits.

Feel Human

A second passed me by, and in that instance there was a miracle. A blessing disguised in skin. She healed my mind with words she said would cure my nervous heart. Unknowingly, she physically manifested salvation. Pulling me from the deepest, darkest pit of self-loathing into light. What she knows is simply external, nothing quite internal. Never would I have known that these walls could be broken down so quick - so secretly. At long last I see myself.

Durden

I've seen starry eyes dyed white.
Drown alive inside wishing hells
and worm wrung skin tempered in
fevers. Flawed to the opinionated
perfectionists who chew on pregnant
tongues.

I was out of mind.
Out of sight.

My tight knuckles balled – knotting rope
to enclose on the tips of pressed lips
split sick. I'd begun the explicit sentence
with foul play, and broken noses. Purple
deep in between a swollen collar, and
city streets skinned with rubber.

Asphalt consecrated in teeth and pieces
of denim. My image a mess. Beaten, busted,
bleeding, gloriously defeated with victory.

Astral

The thin sheets between
 us hold no secrets.
Projecting illustrations to
map out imaginary streets,
winding open worlds to
unfold miracles at
each milestone.
We're sleeping,
floating, wandering
carelessly through stormy
skies cooking lightning.
Two unconscious
passengers scaling the
moon and sun, to reach
armored heavens.
One blessing at a time, said life.
One lesson, one strike.
We top pyramids,
we mount mountains for levitation.
Picking prayers from the atmospheric
web to be read like letters.
Soul notes to be returned
with interventions.
Swallowing mouthfuls of
ambition, we scream –

Carpe Diem! Carpe Diem!
Carpe Diem!

Gravity

This dirt smells of old fire. This room,
in her voice feels less dark. Sleeping with
the incubus, I follow the night into dawn,
washing my flesh in rivers, in volcanos, in
hurricanes, and tsunamis.

I think of rooftops. Windows, busy streets.
I think of deadbeats selling advice. Of the
spinning world. Of soured sex.
Of life, love and death.

How the mice,
the roaches,
worms, beetles,
blue moons, lampshades,
color televisions,
books, notepads,
this bed, and
gravity all communicate.

Of beggars on Broadway Boulevard.
Of town cars hydroplaning into cash bars.
Of legs sweating perfume.
The shadow smoke, acceptance speeches.
Clapping hands, and trophy stands.

Through my secrets you browse,
little snippets on preview.
Come inside, come inside.
Inside out I'll love you.

3rd Wheel

Crooked teeth
cranked spine
swollen fingers
spent mind.

Twisted gut
splintered skin
swallowed grins
sheltered in.

choking up
spitting rust
thinning buff
fucking love.

3rd wheel
just as usual
fuck it all
I'm the usable.

Beautiful This Way Comes

I met her in a café downtown. Exactly when
the long hand landed seven. Alone, she'd been
sitting with starlit eyes holding dreams, and
reflecting back magic. Kismet conversations
over microphones, atop rooftops and well into
sunrise.

She told me how beauty befell the earth
and of open minds meant for worth.
Kindred spirits - she and I shared dreams
and spent pasts of worlds, and vast knowledge.
A sweet, unique mix. 6 weeks passing and I'm a
heart lift on stereo rifts, temping my jukebox
blood to dance with her rhythm. Soundly
talented, alive inside the lines of her grin
exhaling serendipity.

Entranced in moments found for making,
I allowed her the key to my keepsake.
Something out of a silent movie.
With all the colors, popping out the black
and grey. Spot lit silhouette casting mirages
of her frame.

Still in motion, I could feel the room spin
around commotion. But she remained, and that
moment continues to circle like a record to the
recorded beat of conscious. The way she kept
swiping her glare, mesmerized I ensnared her stare.
I knew if she too had insight inside this wild
fire of mind, I too could make her mine.

And we connected on levels, on plains, on pages,
in space, in scenes, in screens. And when I look at her,
I feel peace.
A heart starter.
A starter of heart.
She's a musician of
God's grand art.

Southern Fleshes

Unfolded, she laid holey,
19, on main street as an
elemental elegy of the
elegant.

Naked in the color shot
sky, she was the best of
flavors.

Her gutter gold grain
filmed in southern fleshes.

Animalistic Science

We hid our shadows around lit fires of open nature.
With mother earth and all her pleasures inside a
silhouette stowaway. I watched the brown planets
in her eyes revolve, twist and turn just as heartbeats
rotated gravity. And held her waist, bones and face
inside that space bed of ultimate duplicity.
With harmony and fire mixing, she tames my nervous
storm to install a calm. Partaking in counterpart
charm, she lies down to bathe mutuality, and the
explicit science of our animalistics. Still caught
between my fingers, I smell her will, her love,
passion, commitment, loyalty. The intimate levels
of completion, arousing an awakening to begin.
Off the end we dive, tucking and rolling, grabbing
and pulling. Our teeth marks leaving behind scars to
clothe our untamed hearts.

She's an exquisite paramount of longevity.
This deep to surface with sensitivity. She's a
kill shot eradicating hurt. A vicarious scream
weaved within wants. I see I'm where I belong –
in this pod built of two naked souls. I held her
weight atop, and breathed her in like menthol.
It wasn't enough, I couldn't find satisfaction of
the flesh she fashioned from the lips of God.
I just inhaled, feeling all her wet ends
compromise every flaw I had. Wrapped in revelations,
I found a new scripture written inside the lines
of her thighs. One for resurrection, one for
salvation. One for the declaration of
subliminal solitude.
This earth quaking sunrise tilts until
the sleepers sleep, dreamers dream, and
lovers love. Our miracle is those of many.
Harmonizing chemistry to realign the fervor.

A fuck away from igniting the night.
A touch away from control. Tonight
we'll feed wolves to sheep, and
eat the moon whole.

2.0

I dreamt of
avalanches
piling down
in waves of
the noir
narcotic,
in rage
to bleed
the straight
edge. Count
me in, count
me all over,
I'll pull you
in and romance
you under.
Squeeze my
bones make
me a believer,
press your lips
to the loaded
receiver.

We, The Playful

There we were, locked in position. Her legs over mine, fingers tangled. Lips pressed to exterminate distance. She's a tease, a playful romantic lover chewing at the end of my tongue, sucking dry the color. I felt her wetness in my mouth, her nurturing nature to extort sensual nerve. I dried her spit with mine, and thumbed the smooth line of her chin. Her heat pushed me to counterattack. Sending waves and vibrations to swell beneath my core. She hadn't known what she had done, she just sat stroking the length of her hazel hair. Eyes overly hazed, cheeks burnt in blush and those timid lips quivering. If I would've told her, it would have doused the realization of carnality. I fed her my tongue. Her hand brushing against me. Now she knew. She giggled, snickered, let loose that cute and irresistible charm she bestowed inside. I just sat, biting my cheek, trying to contain myself. Restraining from taking her right there in the center of public view. Fuck it, we'd make a fine specimen to examine. But I withheld, combing back the strands of loose hair behind her gentle lobes, and counted every breath she exhaled with an open mouth.

"Do it."

She said it with such demand that I felt shivers. I had managed to control my mechanics. From toes to fingers, breasts to thighs. Crawling a flavor to explore. We couldn't contain it. She had her head pushed back against the seat, her face in direction. God, I wanted it. I wanted her. Her body, her flesh. I wanted to eat her up. All these illusions floored my imagination when we started towards the city. How she'd bend apart, of the sound to reflect from the floors to walls. The sensation of her depth. Fighting the wheel, I entertained the feverish warmth soaking within the crease of her hip. The photographic reels came spinning behind my eyes again. Flipping through like a sketch book – of her heels to roof, in nothing but great lighting. Her expressions weighing to narrow concentrative brows and eyes of sexual hostility. But it was all in mind, except for her handheld choke working me graciously.

A flood flogged the roads, all roads promised with any
destination of success, and we were left aimlessly searching,
frustration pinning us. She wore it beautifully, and I only
dared to dream of quenching it. I kissed her wrist, fingers and
lips. I needed more, she needed more, but our time was fading.
Foreplay for the century.

This desire is evolving into a craze.
Soon, very soon when the universe
aligns, we'll dance inside one another,
and ignite the fucking hemisphere.

Private Worship

Swollen skies had been replaced with creeping blackness and the atmosphere held vigorous, energetic hormones. Lost from awareness, we had slipped away, vowed out into the seclusive solitude of our own private worship. Whole in our primitive values, we extorted ourselves to find the eccentric necessities we so long craved. One another committed to the practice of each other's secrets. She had many hidden along her curves, to the acoustic recoil of her volumetric requests. All in range of my qualifications. The heat washed the windshield and mirrors, even our slippery silhouettes dancing through a shadow sedation of blissful rocking. Breaking fevers had never pressed out toxins quite like that night, and still I reflect on the sensations of mass strictures reigning away within muscle. Of the shift in climate, of how the tight spaced interior held two vibrantly spastic soul breeders, abolishing time to concentrate on the triggers of pleasure. The aftermath only proposed that we lie awhile to morph into arms, legs, chins, elbows, feet and hearts. Counting every line, freckle, and birth blemish branded into our creative collaboration. She in all her emotions, wore the ether with royalty. A delicate design demanding an encore. Until the sun burnt elastic holes in the oxygen globe, and the trees made appearance, we consistently carried on, matchmaking our bodies to medicate under meditation from behavioral addictions.

Labyrinth

She sat there in a fever,
prolapsing and sweating fire.

Rapturously rounded in warmth,
shedding self-born sins into a
vast valley of verbose epression.

Exorcising suppressions to sell
my soul with, I, compelled to her gist,
fed my price on her roaring soul.

Wired her bones beneath bewitched
secrets, foiled in fanatical resilience,
creased her waxed weight into 6 different
folds and ate her whole.

Love Over Night

The silence. It creeps, crawling
carefully through these walls, up
winding stairs, over the balcony,
through the halls, and into my room.

She, the ghost. Quietly calming
her shade to wither wildly
around my perched breaking.

I can't stand these four
corners. This palace, temple
of stagnant enclosure.

It's suicide.

My neurotic logic contrives
ridiculous fictions of her
being out late with another,
dancing in his covers – spilling
my love on the carpet
like cheap wine.

Kink

I took hanger pins to her nipples, and watched
her squirm blindly, biting roughly, violently
down on the ball stuffing her teeth. She wet the
table, flushing a current to bathe her thighs.
Red, polished pink and raw. Constrained, captivity
confined her kinks.

The way she implemented savage demands,
solid and subtle, just how I imagined, just
how I liked it. She had no say, no authority
or dominance to tease. She could only beg,
whine for my touch to penetrate her deepest
quirks.

Sweet and sour satisfaction streamed
from her mouth. Knees vibrating, arms
shivering - was she coming from anticipation,
or of my throb that slammed inside?

Breaking the barriers of sound,
the clapping storm of whips and chains -
manipulated the atmosphere to jive with
her motive moans. Over and over,
fucking and slapping.

Catching her throat to further pleasure,
I for good measure and fairness unleashed
my girth to replace the bond in her lips
and forced her to swallow.

Her legs quaked as I finished her off,
feeling her tense. Orgasms manifesting
like warfare.

1,2,3,4 - When she rounded 5,
she collapsed in ecstasy.

Testosterone

We see knuckles that are pop cherry
red soaking the bathroom floor.

A man's face flushed in long lost hope,
with eyes beaten blue, bruised all the
way down through his nose and lips.

Busted Reflection, a shattered mirror,
and his chest that heaves in
sporadic formation.

There's a dead man in the corner,
next to an old, cracked,
blood battered tub.

His face is gone, rid of bone
construction and shape.

In his hands we see a switchblade
free of damage.

Back to the man in the mirror,
obviously the victor.

He spits a cord of metallic
with teeth into the sink,
straightens his crooked tie
and exits the washroom.

Mirage

As I lie here after 11:00
flipping ideas of pages.
Of her, her body, hair
within ivory skin,
lips and tongue.

How she slips
asleep to speak
of love.

I imagine an
outline, silver
casing, and
crafted warm.

Her, floating fire
on the peak of a
soaring dawn.

Baptism

On my way out, she decided to go all in.
Wet skin, a spine that panned down into
the folds of what could be baptism.

Undressed, she cocked a glare over,
nipping a hole at the corner of her lip
and slithered into a wave of carbonation.

Clouds rolling above outside
these walls couldn't compare
to the white fuzz leaching
her body.

Legs bent, arms rowed in
reverse, a neck to chin,
teeth licking, loving work
of perfection demanding my awe.

She saw, she knew, giggled and
pulled me in with her and
all that skin.

Salty Captain

If I could open myself up
without the visceral mess,
I'd hand out my emotions
all in color.

And as you roll around soaking the
diversity of blues and reds, pinks and
black, golds into glowing greens, I'll
print photos of you.

Swirling, swimming, and spinning – I'll
make love to you in all that ink.
No one mentioned the making of art
messy, they didn't have to.

She sprawled out beneath me,
slipping wet like an oiled down
mermaid. Five fingered fins,
linguistic lips fit for a sailor.

"Salty Captain" she called me,
slurring sarcastically.

Purity

As we fade in on this empty street of darkened cars and dead city lights, We are inflicted by an intense fear of dread. The thin, light rain sprawling down to pool and pelt against gravel sends a vibe of distant menace and sleeping innocence. We hover above the silent vicinity of nothing suspicious and float upwards so to pass through the heights of over lingering trees. Down we dip, through a neighborhood of half-lit homes – a residence fit for a domestic safe haven. Cars are parked in place on driveways, curbsides, among untrimmed lawns. There stand among the porch side a couple of swaying silhouettes and rambling laughter. Conversational status to the resemblance of college disposition. We pass through their banter and zoom through into the front door, across the occupied den of not so civil, appropriate participates – and find way to the stairway. It leads up, up higher around to another set that winds into a selection of doors. The bathroom ahead that lies open in light to expose a half-naked couple smothering one another. The suave shaved son of explicit behavior has this Barbie doll designed babe perched on the sink, her glossy fingers trailing cuts through his hair, as his are weaving up her skirt. This is the house of sin. Home of sexual expedition. The next room is no different, here rolls a band of tangled body parts, ripping the greasy sheets - masked by kneecaps and armpits. Orgiastic at best, and if you're a freak, a play thing, a submissive, dominant dealer – then this here, inside these four walls stocks roost to your vices and niches. This little partition of society doesn't exist in daylight. Dawn dials the neighborhood back into these science projects who pretend to be your doctors, Insurance agents, and white-collar bosses. Even they still hear the naughty, plastic queen whining through the shower wall.

Danger, Danger

From the distance
she moved in an
abstract body of
shimmering gas.
Fluidly shimmying,
flapping her wet bones
to melt into a fog.
And as she splashed,
I noticed the candles
evenly situated
around the rim
of my bed.

This bed,
our bed.

The bed we made
love in. And as
absorbed as I had been,
I knew she was
a bit dangerous.
But I liked danger,
more than I liked
myself.

Friction

I watch her sitting. Length of hair
idling over the whips of eyes.
And in the moment I cannot feel the
breeze, nor the heat sticking sweat
to skin, but only my chest, expanding
to deflate in and out of unison.

Oblivious, she carries her smile to me
with friction. Then is when I realize
that I am the luckiest bastard on this
planet, to know the limits she inspires
within, to touch her, listen to every
word slip through lips and splash away
all my insecurities.

It's like sifting the salt from the sea,
pulling the shine from diamonds.
There is no place, no division, soul
charming enough to ever make me leave.
In the depths of her watering eyes,
rivers brimming over, I pull her into
me, squeezing together our hearts,
and I assure her of this.

I've found the one who conquers my
demons, settles the score of sorrow,
and casts out frivolous fear.
She's made waves in my emotions.
She's picked up the pieces
of my brokenness.

Little danger, little lover,
together, we'll fight for
one another.

Marvel

Freckled and
dressed in
nothing, she
strings a
smile together
with teeth.

And in the
way she loves
to listen,
I'll forever
be the sound
to her sleep.

Nymph

Screaming, I found her sprawled, spine spanned in the center of the room. Legs expanding at each end, toes curling, and the arch of her neck welcoming me through thin eyes. She had the length of rubber rolling between her fingers, in and out, some warming routine to cast out the morning poison. I felt the shiver of cold sweat swell beneath my buttoned wrists, dampening the fabric to bleed a new shade of white. The publicity stunt held at my preview, had her gushing with premediated mass masturbation. Colorfully airbrushed, this porn star acrobat performed her talents like a trained whale would do in front of the media. The more, the more she moaned. The more she tested out the elastic durability of her limits. Swollen already, from pink to blue silicon, pyramid crafted handiworks. All originally selected by her knack in craftsmanship. She'd switch, altering between woods to rubbers, from glass to plastic, as if this experimenting nymph, took her length and quality meticulously. Shoulders curved at the neck, knees just visible below her two, petite pieces of artificiality, she opened her narrow eyes so wide, wider than I'd ever seen. Bulging bolder, brighter, with a mouth slurring slang not fit for parental tyrants of censorship. She opened my imagination. And I'm not sure if it was the way she appealed to me in naked contrast, or the sounds of her abnormal patterns of breathing, but that night I fell in love with female anatomy.

Sheet Eater

It was one of those nights,
with the dims enchanting the
room to a placid hue, the bed
made so that the end of the
sheets were rolled and tucked,
dividing a partition between
the rustled, feathered headrests
and a lounging lady, with her
dirty feet sleeping sound.

She had been here before, needing
a getaway to crash. How could I refuse
a little runaway like her, ebony
curls contacting the cutout of her
healthy hips, bronzing into the
scheme of different colors.

I've always found her to be
somewhat of a kosher vice.

In Sweats

The curve of her wrist,
swatting hair. The tone
of her tongue, shaping
lyrical miracles. The blush
beneath her eyes, spacing
blemish to touch my thumbs.

Sunrise in sweats, she
is my rising sun, with
fingertips drafting
magnets to move heaven.

Before and after the past,
one day we will wear ours
and shed like serpents.

Silver Skin

I'm roaring white lines into the
destination of a silver something.

My hands are heavy hooks, hanging
loose into every awkward
invitation I have ever took.

Look alive, look strong,
look confident.

Erase the disgruntled
makeup you've smeared
in like clay.

It'll make
horror masks look
comfortable, cozy
and cute in all the
displayable dismay.

On rocks, in rows
of all the lights
fighting to glow,
she is the only
brightness.

The only star in a
returning blackout.
A chemical cookbook.
An illusion inside a high.
A composition without
the sketch marks.

All that is good,
without the bye.

Fishblood

Our human warmth.
Our Lazarus lines.
Our faceless skeletons.
Our cryptic creations.
Our sectional shadows
shedding holographic
dynamos of death.
Our latitudes and
horizontal heavens.
Our provocative paranoias.
Our savvy sadism.
Our naval metamorphosis.
Our passiveness.
We are various.
We are careless.
We all care less and less.
We are changeless by change.
We all revolve inward instead
of outward. We are our own
organism of organs and atoms.
We are pending permanent.
We are the parted promises
down the scalp of
dogmatic dominance.
We are nimble and nude,
nude and nimbly nauseous.
We are a globe of ghosts
bullying the haunted.

Exorcism

Living lights light up the darkest
spaces of this lifeless nebulas.

We are the colorless epitome of absolution.

The cathartic epiphanies moseying
and rambling onward through perdition.

We are flaccid and flattened upon our
belly and bones. Nothing is known here –
separated from spirit and spirituality,
sex and sexuality.

We are the sleeping sleepers
designated to a deathless orbit.
We're the lost, lone lovers left
out for discovery.

These flexible bald bodies
are as slick as water.
Eccentric instruments
mimicking the promiscuous.

She's auburn audio, punk and progressive. Like a favorite record, perpetual and invasive.

Howling

This life has been
the best it has ever
been since you came
along. You are
the foundation
to which I frame
pyramids on.

The howling
opaque seas
sailing my
heart home.

I digested a girl who
has always had a way
with claiming my ether,
enfolding the stars,
and inverting the
universe.

Aerials & Anchors

Wild like a dream, she's
kismet and kinetic.

A lucid existence submersing
aerial anchors to gravitate god.

Alive, we're living, aloud,
she's loving.

Coaching starry coasts to
carry away our vessel, out
and above into the plethora
of supersonic memory.

We have survived, endured,
nourished internal infernals
by the weight of heart.

Ever and onward, surmounting
higher upon levitation -
elevating, lingering to
experience the surface
of her romantic halo.

Of her homeland heaven
exhaling beautiful breathing.
Of her sublime ether, revolving
circular around my globe.

She's my moon. She's my solace.
She's my spiritual regime.
She's the stars in the ocean.
She's wild, wild like a dream.

I'd like to ensnare
the arson in her bones,
warm the fire

I only want to build a life in the
God design of her eyes, and live
everyday in absolute vulnerability,
belonging, growing, forming a body,
a prism, a shape, a kingdom, a universe.

She has been ciphering universes.
The skinless abstraction,
the deadly dreamy.

Diamond Dawn

An emerald body of salt splashes fluidly across shimmering sand. Wild, rooted palms dance, bowing down to mingle with the horizon, while an orange iridescent dawn sets the scenic tempo of two walking silhouettes. IVY and LANDO. Their sway saying more than words ever could – their bodily lingo loud enough to magnetize the ocean tides. We hear the laughter, embrace the invisible scent of mutual chemistry, and we walk with them closely. They row their blended wrists back and forth within the whipping wind of passion. And in the moment, they conform to their own spacious, heart-spoiled world, where words slip from mouth to ear, and with eyes to lips they transcend cohesively – wound around one another like breathing fixations. Baptizing feet at the edge of crawling salt, they entertain a spot soft enough to sit. Lando compliments their roost with a couple of branded bottles – comfortably celebratory.

Her words are faint, empty upon the feedback of gusty air, but their alluring, vibrant eyes ponder with deafening delicacy.

IVY - "When we are plains apart, and the sun has no way of reaching both of us, will you still wait for me?"

Lando intimately brings her mold more closely, comforting her question without the need for language.

LANDO - "You better believe that all of my heart, no matter the distance or weight it might endure, will forever belong to where yours beats. This isn't temporary."

He brushes away the shine from beneath her eyes, words becoming transformed into movements, visually bold, colliding into each other with similar force as the bowling, bustling current ahead of them. For a while they rest and attend the audible sensory of everything, witnessing the ascension of a golden radiant globe.

IVY — "I haven't known a single moment since you came into my life, where I felt alone. Even when we are monuments away, your presence remains."

Humans like Ivy and Lando were made gentle. We see their luxurious life, their living love so profound in measure, it is hard to comprehend — to compete with. An entirety of a day is exhausted in the company of themselves, flicking through memories, soundless through time of past to present. We resonate with this reality of hours and years spent separated. Daylight commences to wane, dissolve below the line of sky and sea, and the sight of this seaside dwelling switch into a location of picket houses and parked machines. This is Lando and Ivy ending their day together, their day of connection and realignment. She looks at him, caringly and devotedly — with all the love a universe could conceive. We perceive its power pledge forth a downpour from the hue of her eyes, and we feel the strength within her peel. They share a farewell romance, before a uniformed Lando departs his heart and home to catch his leave.

Over earth we lay, lying out
loud to serpents, and harvesting
holy hells for the rampant
righteous. We are worth no
less than gold. No more
than diamonds.

The angle of
her vessel,
heaven bound.
Glittered in
liquid earth.

The Rabid

A blast of brilliant light
separates the earth and sky.
Filtered gravel garnishing
the glow and grit of glorious
existence.

Surreally sensational,
a sensual scenario.
Sweetly sexual, as she
lies, sleeping before me.

Before me, barely sleeping,
bare and afraid, sacred and
scared. Slimming dead in depths
of discographic segmentation.

She becomes the single
archetypical animal.
The rabid romantic.
The defective atom pending
perilous evaporation.

She implodes spiritually.
She's exposed privately.
She stirs steam and smoke
to stream arousal.
She's white hot.

A hot petite picturesque,
falling to pieces at the seams.
Abducting me savagely,
darling, abduct me violently.

Extract the imagery, all that
is me physically.
I want to be rid of woes, of worlds,
of religion, of existing.
I want the planets to collide – I desire
to taste the finite morph me.

Solar Avenues

These are the avenues of
depleted vital, resolutions
reflecting back streams from
solar heavens - hues spawning
dimensional dreamscapes.

Cosmic showers shatter arid fire.

Warm tongues heating
homeless hope.

Procreative energies let swim
spinelessly through
plasmid prayer.

We hydrate hydra tides,
and sift skinny to skim
debris out of space.

We are the aspirational
astronauts who forgot
to seek oxygen on the sun.

She's a liquorish caged
hexagram praising
seance water.

She's a womb weaver. An earth creature of city sand and midnight shimmer.

IV

FLESH PHOENIX RE ISSUE / MITCH GREEN

Salamander Street

We are the unsavory
scapegoats on Salamander
Street dampening the
domes of the dogmatic dearest.

Raw, Untapped, blistered.

Nosebleed Nadia in bone
mill and burlap - goads
the naysayers to wound
cure the cooing hysteria.

Fair weathered, damned, digested.

Imbibe the ceramic ether,
take home the tide
and rinse off the spine
of secular tumors.

Vile, seductive, infested.

Floating teeth biting fluorescent
echoes in the darkest lofts of a pith.

Rancorous, sultry, persuasive.

Explicit evidence of the evident turmoil;
sipping rifts from wrists of the afterbirth.

Coagulated, alive, murderous.

Nothing human sleeps
on Salamander Street.

Glass Flames

Eternal serpents in glass mouths,
moves the brooding ambrosia to
scream out in shallow breathing.

Like moths to flames, we are
becoming fiery flint on the crown,
arousing creational slaves,
salivating salvation, foaming
rabid - a thousand miles over,
underneath the breath of
depravity.

Hands down the pants
of the ominous, scourging slander
to dissect the posh pricks of a
generation.

Contagious and courageous
we are the brooding mated devils.

Larva Hearts

Stranded, suspended,
delirious and leveled,
wastelands lay parallel
like coffins carved
inward leeching our
larva hearts; we are the
capsized impressions
haunting the whitewashed

Amen avid figments,
marred blue, scar out marvels.
No more than caged up
catastrophes chewing
on laced wallpaper - high as
the heavens, we thawed at
room temperature.

All figured out,
we were all murdered out,
with no land left to leave,
no one left to love,
only a fistful of hair, and
black blood.

We were so fucked up.

Jargon Hounds

This sensory stagnation of
being weightless, atop the cavern cold
summits saturated over foiled
ends. Harvested from root to heal,
nautical nomads stain
revelatory sky gates.

Blistering blasphemy bakes
bone dry the chastised,
holed up in the transient
matter of humanoid paranoia.
Bawling human clay,
shapeshifted and shrink-wrapped.

Prowling poltergeists siphon
the evangelical ether,
submerging blue, jargon maniacs
swimming naked in parasitic pools.
They engulf the gulf dividing raw woods.

Blood bloated insects, we swarm
and savor the feverish as
we warm our flesh on the sun.
It blows oval until we are red
meat - the sophisticated market lamb.

And just like hounds
to blood, we stalk the wire.
We creep clairvoyant mages
into the terrain of malice.

All strung out, secluded to space
away the near and far. A witchy, ginger
clout entity, knees to chin,
nostrils to ivory, nourished
from the dermis. Spelled on, the

ribs of hounds caved, and the red
witch burnt her mouth on the sun.

Mice transform into lions,
wolves into men, men into rats -
until evolution mates with
mutation, and originality sours.

But we will govern growth from the
inside out, poisoning immortality
just enough to bribe the red witch,
who strangles just enough to get off.
Shivering, double vision.
Wet between the knees.
Inverted at the dome, she
chokes on the visceral cord.

Like hounds to hunger, we devour,
and our ribs too will cave.

Mammal

She is the arid absence of secular lanes
along an open cavity. A lost girl, colorless
amidst all the city lights swapping
pinholes to pierce nakedness. I felt
frigid flesh bead up like fins.

A figment of fragility foaming at the gums.
She's a horny, ambitious, violent, noir blessed
mammal who runs with vertical razors to cast
reptilian vines through velvet wombs.

We have damned the forlorn,
just like we have forlorn the damned.
A home like a stable stashing
the spiritually swallowed.

She came to me, caged, caved in iris session.
A temple north of winter; a shell, a skeleton.
Her automatic, anatomic moves made noise like
mad house bedrooms. Vocal, the narrative of
nuance naivety possessed our perception.

Chasing clouds in a darkroom, she savaged
simpleton trauma from outside the lips of pupils.
The spectral seducer, skinned alive, nakedly smelted.

Inverted panoramic pyramids fetch fossilized aliens.
Her exclusion of normality proves paranormal religion.

Roam Atlantis

When we were younger
our faces peeled grey.

God I knew better.
So gravely golden,
gory grace, prey me
a new path to roam.

Inhale hope like hate.
Sway space appendages
to become planets of
their own.

I felt you bury diamonds,
but my dear, those are
burning stars. Scars like
secrets we kept in the dark.

There is distance in
demeanors sifting stray.
Culling the colors of the
bashfully, masterfully
strange.

Asphalt Angel

Dissolve the dependent
glimmer wedged between
a star and the asphalt angel.
Chemical caged carrion,
scorched, a slave to care;
assaulting aerial glory to
solve perplexities, like worms
in wounds, starving
scars staining creation.
Stagnant infinities turned
putrid, party pagans
pardon praying plagues.

Channel a cure.
Channel a change.
Channel the tide to
tow us from the
abyssal cast, a killer.

Close your eyes, hand
me your hands to hold,
I will set fucking fire
to the fear you bestow.

I have grown to fit
these rosy bones,
gnarled together
by a God.

More less than
imperfect, my human
matter lingers closer
to ritualize weary
graves in razor sand.

Blue Bone

The grassroots abduct
a streaky bagged moon
girl, Swooning puddles.

She's a dead heart - head
belting elephants.

A spastic node in damp
knickers hydrating arid
astronauts turned
blue bone.

Artery Apes

Footage of the
faint Ambrosia.

Of oxygen homes
hosting hostage
parties.

Of artery apes,
making Casanovas blush.

Of tan tongue division.

Of nomad pollution and
neighborhood noise.

Of gravel teeth and
gruesome love.

Of back seat sex
sessions with bloody
condoms and nail polish
wounds.

Of wet colored breath.

Of smoky smiles
howling heavily,
heavenly hailing.

Groove Gods

Seasonal bodies dunked under
to douse asunder vanishing
warmth.

We warn the way we roll our
wants to become tradition.

Worried that we may end up
as groove Gods in fertilized
fire.

And even if you go,
I'll have gone - worn
by the worst of you,
forever glued the way
tattoos do.

Megalomaniac

There are some
things I hope to
never feel again.

Like the foreign
anatomy of someone
you once loved.

The decomposition
of identity when
reveries reclaim the
embodiment of
a memory.

The human way of
breaking down only
to transcend again
into something new.

The existential puberty
of knowing that the
language learned by
lovers in strange rooms,
are pleasured by silicon
ponies and the blues.

Crave
MITCH GREEN

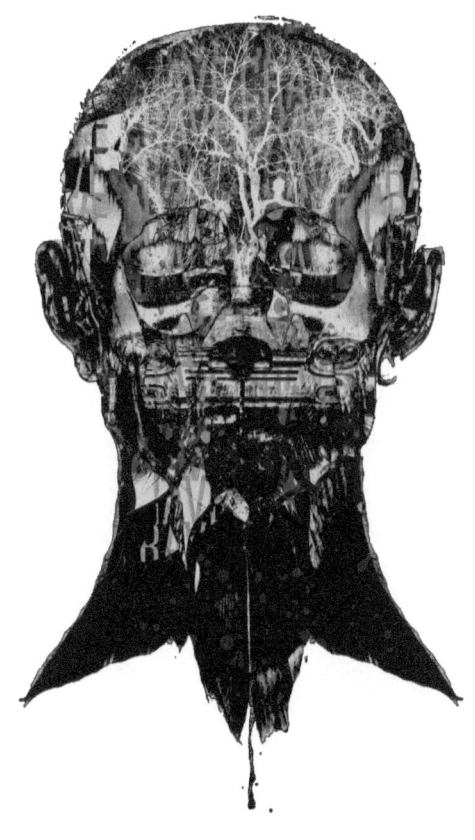

CRAVE
A man's morbid addiction bites back when he attempts to
bury his own personal depravity.
Mitch Green

The short story "Hysteria"
2017

Registered / Copyright: Writers Guild of America, West, Inc.

1   INT. THE WEASEL. A BAR.   1

Dirty rags. barstool legs. Unpolished glasses imprinted lipstick red. A tremoring light fixture. A non-working clock. Bloody napkins. Busted lips. Dirty teeth. Busy hands. Chewing gums. Sweaty collars. Liquid tongues. Bare legs. Wads of money. Gulping throats. Painted nails. Makeup made up women in nothing but false tans, surgically enhanced breasts and swaying hips. Our way, one strides. Weight in mannerism, toting a tray of unpolished glasses. The lipstick red. The dirty teeth. the bare legs. She approaches O. (30's) Battered, strung out. Stabbed with grungy prison tattoos.

Behind now, between the legs of the make up made up woman, we aim up to catch O accepting the unpolished, lipstick red glass. He swabs his liquid tongue across the brim - wiping away the color. Fetish of an animal. He chugs down the frothy substance.

2   INT. THE WEASEL. A BAR. - MOMENTS LATER   2

A woman enters the bar, smoking a half lit cigarette, dressed hardly. In a romper and stockings. Gaudy. Her breasts pressing thimble sized impressions through the fabric. Mysterious but transparent. She ribbons a strand of hair with one finger. With the other, she wedges the outfit up into her divide. A temptress named, SCARLETT (20's) a damsel of disruption. A delicate, dolled up working girl. A make up, made up embodiment of charm and seduction.

Pursing lips. Red hair. Freckles. Collar bone. lipstick. eyes as black as cancer. straight white teeth slipping against a snaking tongue, budding out to strangle attention. Sex surrogate. A vain vixen in pale heat. Over across the room she looks. Sighting O.

She bashfully, boldly brings her body over to where O sits. Flashing open her cleavage.
More drinks. More wads of cash. more dirty teeth. more busy hands. More gums chewing. More busted lips and bloody napkins. More bare legs. More lipstick red glasses. More

More liquid tongues later, and Scarlett and O are seen leaving The Weasel.

3   INT. CAR - DRIVING INTO AN ABYSS OF BLANK SPACE   3

Golden lights. Diamond road. Outside, a blank ether of space. Fish scale stars. The steering wheel dented by O's fingers. A pretty, pale passenger. Tantric tension. Curled lashes and glassy eyes. Darker freckles. Fair flesh. To the left, we steer, off of diamonds and onto dirt.

Crossing inside a border of grey trees mooning overhead we are submerged in motion. Colored fingernails grazing chill-bumps to surface. A lit cigarette bleeds smoke. Rolled down windows escaping air. Windy waves flooding in to blow back red hair. White teeth, caging a liquid tongue from roaming.

The caramel sand. The blank ether of space. The pretty, pale passenger all in nothing beneath thin cotton. An evocative, edgy idol fondling plastic packaging. A condom. She snags a tear by biting.

The car veers to a stop behind a screen of secrecy.

4   INT. CAR - MOMENTS LATER   4

Green radio. White teeth. Liquid tongues. Curling toes. Painted fingers. Lipstick red condoms. Lipstick red cigarettes. Dark freckles. Wet red hair.

Invasive. Drawn into the throes of chaotic chemistry between the two. A performance of arousal quaking the vigorous commotions of carnal connection. Alive, they are alive, lively eccentric - howling life.

Bodily war rages back and forth. Damaged, orange and damp hair appears like rope tangled around Ollie's knuckles. Disheveled, Scarlett's cherry red lips are smeared, wiped past her cheek. Tugging between their private positions - Intervals of their
rowdy, rambunctious momentum at last diminishes to a grunting, groaning, pumping halt.

5   EXT. WHERE NOTHING LIVES - MOMENTS LATER   5

The camera faces from the outside, focusing in on the two through the glass windshield.

Scarlett fumbles her naked breasts into the cotton palms of a bra, while O sits perched with his left elbow on the car door - exhaling a storm of smoke. The aftermath stoking silent tension between them.

6   INT. CAR -- CONTINUOUS 6

We blink to view both through the open window - O's arm hogging half the frame. A cigarette hisses at the tip, partially lighting up his face. He steals a final inhale before flicking the pinched stick of fire out into the darkness. O exhales. We perceive the rolling gust of grey, curling to mask Scarlett's semi-bare silhouette situated sitting in the backdrop.

7   INT. CAR -- CONTINUOUS 7

>   SCARLETT
>   *(unwraps a ball of gum)*
>   Don't talk much do you?

O screams silence.

>   SCARLETT(CONT'D)
>   *(rolls the candy onto her
>   tongue)*
>   I've had a time with the quiet
>   types, ya know, like all
>   mysterious and shit. Really gets
>   me all wet. Really fucks me up,
>   but I love it.

Scarlett slightly squirms in place - positioning her legs to boot the dash. Pulls an elastic, chewy cord of pink through her teeth.

Scarlett looks at O with the gum ensnared within her bite. She thumbs on the radio; sharp sounds of shrill static erupt in volume. Revolving the dial, the flickering

frequencies fade in and out in wavering voices and sirens. She switches off the radio.

> SCARLETT
> (Pulls down the passenger
> mirror and finger scrubs the
> lipstick off her teeth)
> Nada.

Scarlett seductively fingers the flaccid gum back between her teeth - sucking the edge of her knuckle with closed eyes.

> O
> (Slams a wad of cash on the
> dash)
> One more.

8   INT. CAR - CONTINUOUS   8

Close up on Scarlett's throat as she heavily gulps, downing the gum.

9   EXT. WHERE NOTHING LIVES - MOMENTS LATER   9

We glide above, from the hood of the car capturing the steam fogging up the glass surface of the windshield - to the roof where we pause, framing the swaying body of the machine. We see able palms slap and streak visible viewpoints into the interior of the car. Muffled orgasmic wails peak the audible ambience.

10   INT. CAR - CONTINUOUS   10

We are re-joined with the couple inside. The camera captures segments of indescribable body parts; legs, hips, lips, teeth, fingers, hair - and mobile muscles flexing underneath tightened skin. Another episode of carnal seizure constricts at where they connect. Climax.

Again, Scarlett's expired cosmetics are worn - smothering

her pearly starched teeth; the red bleeds pale peach. She shows us her greasy tongue waging like a dog. Devilishly disgusting, but deliciously addictive.

O lingers above, stasis and stargazing into Scarlett's bodily expression. Wound around him. Coiled like wire - softly blushing his waist.

O remains, and we watch his hands trail the sweat glazed consistency of her mold. Up around her thighs, passing the ridges of her ribs, cuffing to crawl over her blemished breasts, riding along the edges of her curved shoulders, and gently swaddling the girth of her neck.

> SCARLETT(CONT'D)
> *(Gritting a grin)*
> Rough player. Gonna teach me a
> lesson? I like it rough. Fuck me.

From behind the two, the camera captures Scarlett's legs blooming wide. Seen as if O is adopting a pair of knee high wings. The shadow figures reflect slightly from the traces of moonlight dawning in.

II   INT. CAR - CONTINUOUS   II
We zoom in intimately on her quivering lips and stretched eyes.

We direct O's quaking hands as they fold and grip around the plush muscles of her throat. Tightening. Constricting to choke. The composure of a maniac enriches his once placid demeanor.

She's uncomfortable. She's lucid. She's frightened. She's panicked. She struggles to get out from underneath. To catch breath from beneath.

A violent tantrum commences, conspires and ends with the cold cadence of Scarlett frozen in his hands. Lifeless.

12   EXT. FRONT OF CAR - CONTINUOUS   12

The brilliance of reflecting headlights dim to death.

13   INT. CAR - CONTINUOUS   13

Back inside, O sobs, cradling her naked ghost. He's dead inside. Detached from reality, he lays Scarlett down so that her head rests at the window and her feet splay out in his lap. Dirty toes, soles as dark as dirt.

14   EXT. OUTSIDE OF CAR - MOMENTS LATER   14

The camera catches sight from the front of the car. The driver door pops open, simultaneously chiming on a low-grade light, faintly brightening up the vehicle.

O elbows out, barely bare, slicking back the sweat and hair from his face. He's a shadow, a figment of grey matter. A devil in contrast with the gritty nature rooted beneath him. In front of us he slices shape through the lights to the passenger door, snatching it open.

Scarlett's body slides midway out of the interior. Her hair's like blackened vines. Her milky arms are like gentle weights. Elastically, she's lifeless, like stone, poised facedown.

We are magnified close on her body. Dark freckles. Slick scars. Red hair. Home tailored heart and script tattoos. Curled lashes and fair flesh. A dead ghost.

15   EXT. WHERE NOTHING LIVES - CONTINUOUS   15

From the inside looking out, face up in back of the trunk, O towers above us. A charcoal cutout. A charcoal killer in long legs and reaching arms. Like grabbing the camera, he pulls back an arrow ended shovel. Like the devil. Primitive gritty, slathered in lipstick red.

A lewd scenic. A dead earth. A dead ghost. A devil in

dirt. A make up, made up murder under fish scale stars.
All in frame, we capture colored fingers. Wet red hair.
Dark freckles risen from gravity.

Suspended, O cradles her chilled core into blank space.

16   EXT. WHERE NOTHING LIVES - CONTINUOUS   16

Jolting jabs of a spade, stabs holes into soil. Carving
ditches. A void. Seven feet beneath the surface. O is a
mutt shedding grit. He reels Scarlett's corpse in, into
his arms, into the void he has carved.

A Beat.

Ariel shot, above about ten feet directing down onto life
and death. Two charcoal humans. The dead ghost with red
hair and dark freckles lies atop. O holds her intimately,
fading to sleep.

17   EXT. WHERE NOTHING LIVES - MINUTES LATER   17

Behind O's eyes, we ingest life. A POV of godly bark
monuments bending overhead by roots. A brilliantly bright
oval planet splicing light. The fish scale stars
peppering an ether. The red crown of a dead ghost.
Tarnished fingers. Digested dim. Darkly damp and ditched.
Dirty teeth. Blackened lips. Twitching toes. A stark
supernatural. Scarlett shudders. She sheds grit. Alive.
Alive. Alive. Reanimated.

O's yellow eyes. His lizard tongue lashing loud sound.
Whining terror. Her rancid, razor wild teeth carves a
ditch. Red dead ghost with lipstick red teeth. Gore girl
in earth blood. Eaten alive, O peels off her red head, and
scampers out of the void. Out into the open orifice of
nature. Out towards red and gold light.

The red ghost flickers behind. Charcoal cadaver in dark
freckles. Purplish, bluish, bare. Digesting the abyss of
blank space. Dirty teeth. Open skin. red turned black
hair. Nearer. Nearer. Nearer.

18   EXT. WHERE NOTHING LIVES - CONTINUOUS   18

A shot of fresh dirt begins to boil with uprooting knuckles. Pounds of flesh blanketing the frame. Female figments birthing. A dozen dead ghosts'. They gather to commune, shocking O into tears. This is his hell on earth. A posh, pink purgatory.

He fumbles. He crawls. He scatters inside the car.

19   INT. CAR -- CONTINUOUS   19

Busy gritty hands. Gritty arms and legs. Shedding filth. Panicked. O looks like a nightmare. A defeated devil. A devil wrists deep in strewn denim and silk. He sifts the clothing for flashing, clinking keys. A panicked nightmare finding them underneath a condom. Lipstick red. Tremors bend his tarnished fingers. Trembling he twists the ignition. The engine strains. Dead ghosts' are all around. Slick and colorless. Charcoal bled. Gore girls in earth blood.

Gums chewing. Jaws like bear-traps. Arms like baseball bats, abusing broken glass. Pounds of flesh inhabiting the ether. Trapped in a claustrophobic coffin. Digesting space. Flooding they suffocate O. Dead ghosts' carving carnal voids. Dirty teeth. Tarnished hands. Liquid tongues. A charcoal sermon. A posh, pink purgatory baptizing a liquid war.

20   EXT. WHERE NOTHING LIVES - CONTINUOUS   20

Ariel shot, above about ten feet directing down onto dirty dead ghosts.

                                            FADE TO BLACK

The Monolithic

The hideous opaque wisps -
inhabiting the vacant abodes
burrowed and buried infinities
deep; the monolithic.

Mayday. Mayday.

The paper-thin gorgon, lain
in cocoon oceans - skimming
velvet shores to seize apparitions.

Doomsday. Doomsday.

Dizzy, dystopic and carnal;
strewn, shipwrecked inside.

Repent. Repent.

Viciously vicarious, born again.
Slow dancing in torched rooms;
hazmat skeletons.

We Mothered An Apparatus

We were the punk youth.
The adolescent bloomers'
coerced and coaxed to be
these Subtle, opinionated
monarchs.

Obsessed with the perpetual
epitome of death and faith,
we were fixed on the
fascination of how it
depicted philosophical
dimension Into our
cerebral locker of
mystery.

Invincible, we thought
we were; climbing high,
seduced by immortal naivety.

Some provocatively wild
wormed species spawned
into a stratospheric
ball of oxygen.

And in the end, in this
slithering stark grace,
we mothered an apparatus.

Black Sheep

Lair layers pledged to babe the
iron orifice. Salacious shadows
in dormant doors shelling projected
disturbances down to wire tissue.

The neurotic son.

Poignant to be frigid behind
barrel sable bulbs - debauchery
delves damply, paddling soles to
disrupt a velvet disaster.

The erotic one.

A flushed fiasco - coexisting on
the belly of sobbing dames; duplex
grimaces in gaged ruin.

The black sheep blood.

A Forest

Up and down, down and up we go.
I can't seem to get it right.
The consistency thickens at
the back of your eyes, your
voice, so coagulated with the
poison I dose you up on.

Always beneath the surface.
Suffocating, still, I have
given out of breath.

Adapted to exist within the
paranormal color of blank space
we explore with fertile faith.

In your hair, a forest.
It feeds me in, just like
the way you do, while
under the weight of all
I am; a camera, developing
negatives.

Coiled And Healing

Undone down to wire frames shaking off scales
– we could always breathe easier inside closed
cars hiding idle tongues inside backseats.
Confessional booths to splay us out; where we
would talk about our dreams becoming droughts.
How in each place we left our mark, could be the
place we would find healing.

So pour me under your lids, i'm
swimming to drown, cause' I
haven't felt a spirit so sound
until the day I found you around.

We all dance on glass shells to document our
existence. All careless and colored crazy,
we've made a promise to keep us together. A
heavy home resting on the eyelashes of your
sleepy savior; I've given into giving you my
life. There will be a plot of soil saved for me
and you.

Cause' last night I found your spirit living
in our sacred places, coiled and healing.

NSFW

Crank up the clairvoyant mages
bent in cages, who've been on the
heel of my chin chanting charm to
the channels of plagues. Pitching
age into life, living minute to the
hour On recoiling nuance noise.

All in a spiritually foreign language.
Lacerate the lament, lick the acidic
aura off of arousal. Stream the veins
of maleficent monoliths. Violate the
wanting with sensual strain. Spank
the splinters out from lavender
lungs getting high and haunted by
dissecting damage.

Neurotic

The pyramids have all become inverted
crypts safe keeping sacrificed air.

Silver linings coat the base of lips
like an abyssal film. There is no room
left to leave our arms open.

Like lifting, we soar, steal the glow
of God to become one. Snuff smothered
in our ambient grotesque, we morph
into division.

Neurotic and naked,
we are planet divorce.

Chemical Disaster

I've seen you fade black to sunlight,
a product of promise, broken at the
heel of hope. We were always running
away from shadows just to fall back
to the home we pledged to never call
ours. There lies beauty in those
cancerous nights where we stayed up
fighting back fears that in time
severed our comfort.

On and off, we would be, mad at the calm
raging war behind summer eyes sweating
truths. I was never the best of anything.
Hardly the best of us, and when the warmth
of you finds place far from mine, I feel
the depth of weight burrow in. Press deep
to hurt.

A chemical disaster breaking my
melodic brain. I've been beneath
this; kicking and swinging, biting
and punching from the blink of
birth.

Still, I can't seem to decode
bliss, or even hold onto happiness.

We're all really just sad people
faking smiles while moving in place.

Fossils

We've been known to zone out on giving in. Thinking of how we would be the ones to make it past these country roots to find city crowns. Bated down to the end of our lines, we are the used up miracles abused by touch.

The open verses recanting venoms that numb nerves.

But somehow we have become the paralyzed spirits stuck rotting behind the doors that we had built to grow with. Never did we ponder on becoming fossils.

Peeper

Avenues dug out around a tranquil pivot of plasma. An oblivion of water. The circular crater casting blue skin to skim the surface. Neon strobes stain and sting the glass hood. Digested behind the ray of dashing lasers, lie the groping palms of a mid-thirties stranger, swollen in mystery. His misty iris frames, bold, pressing down into the bone of nose. His paranoid flesh pinches blasts of daggers to scratch, and scathe smears into carnal color.

The igniting gusts of illuminate showers spread waves of vibrance to bathe the night in bleach. This is when we see a body casted in glory. Vertically, horizontally, wholly dedicated to natural surrender. Fiber-thin, gracefully gravitational to the pull of the moon. Soundly shaming two fingers to wander wild. Intune with self. Oblivious to the knowledge of the stranger behind glass previewing her intimate routine.

Peeping, pondering to transfixed obsession. Warm words slithered off the white tide of her tongue like the performance of oral practice. Possessed on wind. On wires levitating her complexion to come in birth of pleasure. Spine spanking the earth – her knees seize in sweats. Her soil wrists become worms, ankles spin into snakes. Her lips suck like leeches – and her heart a tumor.

The stranger gasps. A mouth as wide as the sliver between her, spawning gushing gravel. Another sonnet of copious color wipes the scene. Aborting rapture.

Holey

She's the blushed
bloody bod of ghost
smoke. The heavy
heeled harlot,

Wholly hexed holey.

Peach

She's the peach porcelain
procreation of seduction -
skinning scars in skimpy
tube socks. An armageddon,
retro vibrant, vibing smash
single. A darling
dimensional, dabbed at
the lips by evocative thumbs.

Catalysts

There was something about the night we both became catalysts. There was something about how we began just how we had begun. Starting with words. Then with chemical tango. Then with lyrical lingo. Then with the carnal sessions of possession.

It wasn't ever a lie on How we both became so caught up in habitual rituals that we lost Sight of what we were. With a fistful of hair, her demeanor swam circles Around my gospel poverty. She kindly killed the worst parts of me Beautifully.

And I find myself lost in the bizarre bliss of it all. but I'm still A burnt out suicide, seduced by romance.

Exoskeleton

The singular separation
between you and I.

Spastic sexual spectrums
color our arousal to strip
the exoskeleton off of
the fragile honesty our
bodies sweat.

Diamond hips and blush
burnt cheeks are scraped
against the grain of my
intimate.

The way that I savage my
wet tongue to dry the
flesh river gushing from
your spirit.

Milk And Mud

In the depressions of beauty
there is a radiant warmth.

A community of breathing
beings molded out of milk
and mud.

Their celestial stigma stains
the atmospheric cosmos in
sworn Seduction.

Their words sync to the
rhythmic cries of our human.

Their lyrical libido sailing
softly amidst an oceanic entity.

Urchin

We unfolded our layers
to bake brightly dead
below the urchin dirt.

We once were one – sworn
bare and narrow before
duality.

A filthy, fucked up duo
scrubbing out each
other's devils.

Lady Nature

Softly solid, lady nature
salivates; swallowing live
grenades to swell into a
storm of metaphorical muses
mating with cannibal Gods.

Escape

Escape. Escape. Escape.

Find a way far from the place
we came. She said to write her a
love story on how it gets easier
to become warm within these cold
currents.

But my God, my memorial mapped
mind has married the marooned –
and I have burnt the paper pages
that have cut me out.

We never meant to mean the harsh
sounds we made, as our hands flew,
holding blood.

Escape. Escape. Escape.

In the end we appeared dirty and
dizzy from our dance with the devil.

Here There Be Vultures

This deranged dystopian. This homeless housing. This evocative revelation. This hogtied, tender tonged flesh fetish – loaded and whiplashed raspberry red.

A velvet violence. She's a velvet vortex. A carnal cavalry caught cumming wastelands.

Incubuses And Incubators

Sated and stolen in stale
spaces - i'm sorted simple.
Cumbersome demeanors waste
walking dangerously to strain
and stain the skin in shades
of personification.

exploration, immaculate
majesties, romantic
travesties spiking
reincarnation, I lure
the allure of reaction
to nurture natural,
neurotic frequencies.

Constellations and
tranquil depravity.
hypnotherapy and
psychosocial anatomy.

Blank Bodies

And it is so that these blank bodies
are built from the inside.

Cerebrally, morally, spirituality,
we are all fostered by fractions of
coagulated energy, and aren't defined
by laws, religion, God, or man – but by
conscious growth.

We must evolve and surrender to the
notion that it is by our own doing that
we have become this cultivated culture.

This feared formation of human. This
depleted, degenerated definition of a
generation.

We are a reflection of animal.

Bully Queens

We hear the concentrated silence.
We witness the distilled documentation
of existed presence.

Petrify at the nodes of red, green, and
yellow that *flash. Flash. Flash.* Intrude
on Slumber Street, where hopeless homes
are slumped in darkness.

We bully lead bulbs to stab the night – to
disembowel the vast void of puking light.
we're the double lines scoping secrets,
and are the fleshed earth, bare of essentials
 – streaking in bashful spaces.

We tread on human painted pavement.
Blushing with youth, splashing, spawning,
slaving in scenic prey.

And then there are these cherry queens,
the ones with red cheeks, who catch fire
just to finger their flames.

The Sadist

Sequence one installs incarnation. It is redemption, beading stampedes of salt. Sweating signatures of silhouettes we obsess.

We see these fainting fawn legs lounge over knuckle stone knees. Polished in fish-oil, her squeaky, slathered stigmatic psychology strains scripture into her sadist grain.

A miracle carved out of pigmented isolation. An advisory warning to those less of thick skin. Vintage virgin with a tongue severed down center to pleasure double.

She's every morale your mother taught you to distrust. Every organ you swore to never fuck.

She'll swab your soul in serrated glass – and swallow sworn segments of your carnal curated mass.

Lucid Lucy

We begin as nothing near alive.
A venue of deserted earth hung
in arid glitter, disrupting a
toxic nexus.

Nose to mouth, between breathing,
her lips lyrically drive sleep to wet
the back of our eyes.

lucid Lucy – the snuffed ghost,
crowning pale snakes.

Death Sex

The aftermath of thick sex smothers death –
while the young-blood youth who lie within
the lines of their lizard layers lap up
post-rapture.

In our matter, there are, benign blemishes
scuffed by nicked lips. Nudity. Bones and
teeth. Sleek suited secretions. Laced up
rubbers tied taught around the wet heels of
a lover. Some latex spent wasted inside the
curiosity of a grin. her pressed cheeks. The
way she swallows. The way night and day
dresses and bares her.

In her matter, there is innocence to
experiment.

Pink

Pink flesh bleached her teeth.
She is the muffled nuke, nude,
and knuckle gouging grooves
into her slip.

A betwixt image, beaten blush -
swollen and spanked salty.

Maiden

Frail. Delicate. Fragile. Faded.
Fucked. Washed. Whipped. Bled.
Spent. Bent. Purple. Pale. Wet.
Soaked. Split. Scarred. Shattered.
Sheltered. Stripped. Bashed. Bare.
Bold. Exposed. Open. Tender.
Timid. Tamed. Taunted. Sensual.
Starved. Filthy. Aggressive.
Violent. Selfish. Disgusting.
Damned. Tainted. Spoiled. Vile.
Vain. Consumed. Controlled.
Created. Animated. Electric.
Invasive. A reverie. A Martian.
A maiden in mascara.
A murderous miasma.

The Killers

Pull your shape over mine,
light your wick. Because
tonight we are endless.
We're
The sinners.
The killers.
The lovers.
The healers.
The masters.
The makers.
The saviors.
The feelers.

Safe Places

I would take you anywhere with me.
To any unfamiliar landscape scraped
of security.

Just you, me, and the fault line
romancing a beaten horizon, wounded
by our iris ambition.

Where the spectral summit of solace
deserts lifeless ache, lasting to low
the tide - where longevity lingers
loudly in the echoes of time.

Safe places that heal the
scabbed and seething.

BOOK DESIGN
RADPUBLISHING.BIZ

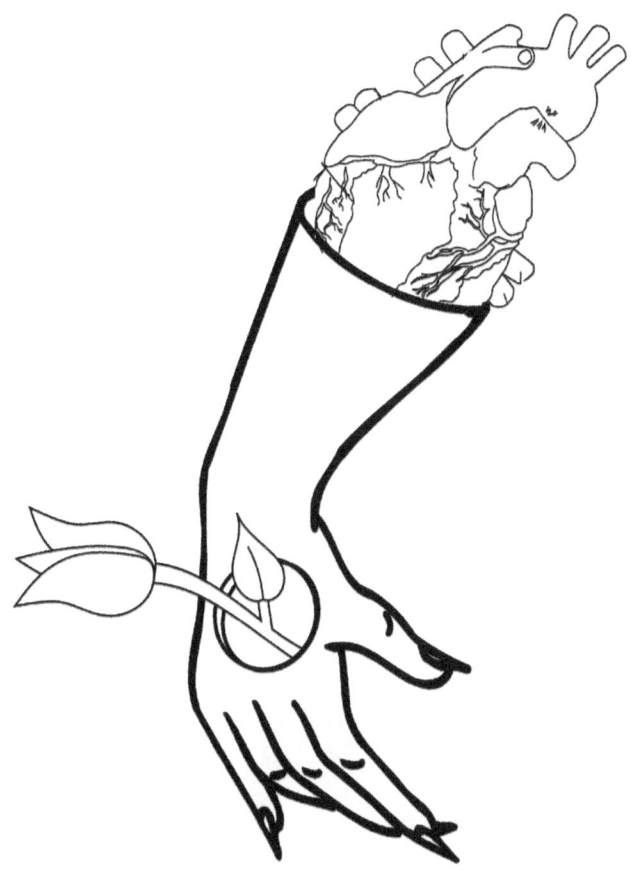

A SPECIAL THANKS TO ALL THOSE WHOM HAVE SUPPORTED MY ART

www.ingramcontent.com/pod-product-compliance
Lightning Source LLC
Chambersburg PA
CBHW032039290426
44110CB00012B/879